EMAIL INBOX MANAGEMENT
How to Master Your Inbox with Etiquette

PATRICK X. GALLAGHER

DEDICATION

I would like to thank and acknowledge the following people for inspiring me to write and complete this paperback book.
My immediate family - you know who you are!

ALSO BY THE AUTHOR

LinkedIn Secrets Revealed: 10 Secrets To Unlocking Your Complete Profile on LinkedIn.com

Publishing a Book on Amazon: 7 Steps to Publishing your #1 Book on Amazon Kindle in Minutes!

Love or Hate Email...21 Rules to Change Your - I Must Check my Email Habit. Get Back to Work and Make Money Again!

Build Your Own Living Revocable Trust: A Pocket Guide to Creating a Living Revocable Trust

Spirituality in the Workplace: A Study Guide for Business Leaders

Amazon Secrets Revealed: How To Sell More Books on Amazon.com

Trapped in a Meritocracy: Cracking the Meritocracy Code - Get Paid More for Valued Performance

TABLE OF CONTENTS

TABLE OF CONTENTS (CONT'D)

SOURCES - Further Reading and Reference Books

Recommended Websites for Further Review

Other Books by the Author

Questions or Comments?

About the Author

ACKNOWLEDGMENTS

This book was born and is dedicated to all my current and future Amazon Kindle e-book fans.

PRAISE FOR EMAIL INBOX MANAGEMENT

"Thank you, Patrick, for finding the motivation and inspiration to publish this practical, hands-on book! It is evident now, more than ever, that busy professionals must change their habits from being Email Junkies to collaborating, problem solving, thinking and creating for businesses to move FORWARD. A must-read for recent graduates as well as current email users who are finding themselves locked in their inbox." - **Paige Webb**, Productivity Specialist, **The Effective Edge**.

At first glance, I was dubious about this book. Email is so simple... what could I possibly learn. I was SO WRONG! After putting into practice the tips and tricks that Patrick outlines I have massively cut down on the amount of time spent handling my emails.

Patrick provides straight forward examples and free tools you can use to speed up and track the email process.

My only regret is that I didn't read this book earlier. I highly recommend that EVERYONE read this book, and that employers makes it a part of their induction reading for new staff. The time/cost benefit of using Patrick's RWEF system for handling emails is staggering. - **Jamie Cawley**, Publisher & Writer

As a developer I get inundated with emails from clients, Managers and business analysts. I used to spend so much time processing email I often had to stay at work late to action them. Since reading and following this book I have developed a plan that has enabled me to priorities and process my email more efficiently and faster. My email accounts (personal and professional) are now far less cluttered. The tips provided in the book are very good and the additional videos and resources were extremely helpful. I will definitely recommend this book to all my friends and colleagues.

- **Janak**, Amazon Reviewer

I am a very busy Mum running around managing several businesses and this book came out just in time. I read most of my email on my Smart Phone and the book included tips on managing multiple email accounts. It's a current event Email Management book that will make you a smarter business person/professional.

- **Becky**, Amazon Reviewer

I bought this book because I was spending more and more time reading and writing email. I often went home feeling like I spent too much time processing email.

This book has 21 chapters that help you develop and plan, so you can process your email in a faster way. I gave the book 5 stars based solely on the additional videos (there was even one in there from Bill Clinton) and the Outlook tip for cleaning up daily email conversations in seconds. Thanks to the author for getting me back my time, so I can spend more time being strategic in the office and taking time for the family at home!

- **Robert**, Amazon Reviewer

PREFACE

Thank you for choosing to read this book. Do you check your email in the office many times per day? Are you an Email Junkie? Chances are that you are hooked on checking email.

An Email Junkie is someone who is hooked on reading, writing and replying to emails as soon as they arrive! I have written this book especially for YOU to help banish this time consuming habit.

With the extra time you will get back from reading this book, you can execute the tasks that will get you results faster. You will undoubtedly get paid more, sooner rather than much later.

This book will help you get out of the habit of checking and doing email each day. You can get back to work and start making money again.

The book comes loaded with help, so you can create an action plan and follow the RWEF email management system. By the time you have finished reading this book you will form a new habit and no longer be an Email Junkie!

Try it today for 21 days and cure your email habit!

Enjoy the ideas shared in this book and create a new habit for your working week! Get faster and more valued in your work hours by everyone today!

INTRODUCTION

"We are what we frequently do" - **Aristotle**

Why You Really Need this Book...

There was a lot of talk in the finance world about saving us all from the *Fiscal Cliff* over the past 6 months. What we really need help with is the **50 Billion Dollar** Email Management Problem! Some say it is much more than that! This book provides 21 rules you can follow to make sure you are not part of the 50 Billion Dollar problem.

Recently in the **USA**, USPS (the US version of the Royal Mail) announced that they were no longer going to deliver mail (post) on a Saturday. Wow! Who Cares I hear you say!!!? How many **USPS customers** actually cared, or even noticed!? You'd be surprised to know - not as many customers of USPS cared all that much. What would happen if companies stopped delivering email?

This change and the constant, "I hate email" conversations helped me move faster to sharing my experience with you in this e-book. I am able to share with YOU my years of experience and training, using Email in the Office. Do you *Love or Hate Email*? Email is a productivity tool that is supposed to enhance your life.

The trouble is, greater than 50% of Email users have never received any formal training for using this Information Technology tool.

Here is a recent stat. about how we use devices to access our email and inbox. Consumers aren't just accessing email using multiple devices. They're also using multiple accounts. Almost three-quarters of US email users ages 25 to 40 managed their email this way, according to February 2012 data from BlueHornet. - eMarketer "Email Marketing Benchmarks: Key Data, Trends and Metrics."

Email Programs

Regardless of your favorite email tool - WebMail, Google Gmail®, Microsoft Outlook®, Thunderbird®, GroupWise® and many others, Email has become a hindrance to improving productivity. Through the use of Email applications tools, or apps. these tools are supposed to make you more efficient. The more times you check your email, the better the chance you will become an average performer.

Love or Hate Email... you need rules and a system you can follow each day that will help you process email to be successful and an expert in that task.

Reading this book, executing the rules for 21 days and more will make you into a **Top Performer**. A **Top Performer** - means you will get the best projects at work and you will go home each day with a feeling of accomplishment. Stay away from the hook of being hooked on "*processing email.*"

How Will this book Help you?

When you leave the office each day, do you feel that you accomplished a lot? Maybe you accomplished a lot because you processed all your email? Sadly that doesn't mean you are getting your work tasks done and getting results fast for your company. What you need is a system that will help you process email quickly and less often.

You also need to realize that email is not your job, it is part of it, but that's it. Running your office from your Inbox will eventually drain you creative spirit. Break the habit by reading and following this book.

Top 10%

Soon you will realize the poor choices you are making, you will find out how the top 10% of performers process email and you will develop a system that works for you. At the end of every chapter [21 Email Rules] you will get an action plan. If you follow this action plan it will move you to the top 10% of performers in 21 days or less!

The Confessions of an Email Junkie!

I couldn't have written this book without the indirect help of numerous people, including my Business partner. My Business Partner asked me one question - Why do you need so many email accounts!!!???

Although I had a great answer, it never explained away the numerous minutes and hours, leading to days I incessantly spent reading, writing, erasing and filing [RWEF] email in each account. Some days this behavior would even take time away from spending quality time with the family and friends. Is that YOU today?

Social Media and the 21st Century

In the 21st century people everywhere, rich or poor appear to be acting like Email Junkies. People are constantly checking their email, or their Facebook® page. Each new friend connects and indirectly sends you another email that you must process. Often accidents happen as a result of not paying attention to what is happening all around you.

Crashing is Bad!

Crashing your car while texting is a good <u>example</u>! We all need to wake up and smell the coffee and be present today. You need to detach from these technological systems that tax and knock the breath of strategic thinking out of you. Read on and learn how you can make technology your tool of choice again!

For every social media platform you have an account with (LinkedIn®, Twitter®, Facebook®) etc. You will also get an Email to tell you have a new follower, or someone wants to connect with you. Net result – even more emails, the split between personal and business emails will depend on how well (or not) you use these email platforms.

Email Stats

The average Email user spends around **36 times an hour checking their email**! Social Media has made this habit even worse! If you are a member of several Social Media platforms like: Facebook®, LinkedIn®, Twitter® etc. you will probably get triple the number of emails. Each social media account will send you a copy of an email for every social media platform you belong to.

That means you will spend even more time checking email on even more platforms/web applications etc. How can you ever get ahead?

What this E-book is not...

This book is not intended to teach you how to use <u>Microsoft Outlook</u>®, or <u>Google Gmail</u>®, or <u>Thunderbird</u> etc. It is not intended to replace all the good information you will find by clicking on your Email Application's Help button, or using your favorite search engine to research a Email Help topic. It's not going to help if you read it and then just go back to your old habits.

Only you can change your habits, this e-book will help you decide and choose what to implement to make that habit a new <u>better</u> habit.

CHAPTER 1 - RECORD YOUR TIME SPENT PROCESSING EMAIL

"What gets Measured gets Managed" – **Peter Drucker**

Time is a valuable commodity

How much time do you spend reading, writing, and erasing email in each sitting? If you are in email all day (meaning you never close the browser, or email application) you are essentially doing email all day. How much time do you think a Top Performer spends in email each day? The answer is the least amount possible.

The 4 Hour Workweek

For some people, like Timothy Ferriss, the author of the "4-Hour Workweek," spends less than 1 day a week doing email. It really comes down to minutes and hours for him. Ok, so he has a Virtual Assistant (Admin) to help him, but the point is that he has managed his work life well. The result - he does as little as possible in his Email Inbox.

You should do the same. If you can't do it for the office email, you should certainly try it for your personal email inbox.

Measure Your Time

Measure how much time you spend processing email. Open up a browser and type http://e.ggtimer.com/ then you can type in your estimated time. See screen shot below – start with 60 minutes. Create a spreadsheet, or use notepad and record 5 sessions of doing email.

welcome to
e.ggtimer.com

Start a timer | 60 minutes | GO! | Options (beta)

Inbox Processing Time Sheet

Create the spreadsheet, something like below. You will see I added 5 rows recording the time for each processing email session. The average in this example works out to be 47 minutes (rounded). You will use this time as a goal later on in the e-book. You must ensure you do not go over your average each day, or whatever period you set aside for your email processing.

	A	B	C	D
1	Session #	Time (minutes)		
2	Session 1	55		
3	Session 2	59		
4	Session 3	30		
5	Session 4	55		
6	Session 5	35		
7				
8	Average	46.8		
9				

Time is Money!

Show your boss how much money you will save by learning an **Email Processing System**, such as the *RWEF* system. You will learn more about this system later on in this book. Share this with your colleagues too. You may not know it, but working for a large company your job is also to help others become efficient in what they do.

You will get a head start, as you are SMART! If you want to be good at email, then you might be better for you to perform the role of an Email Customer Service Sales Representative. Last time I checked via indeed.com the pay was $14 per hour. See [**Figure 1**].

Figure 1.

Email Customer Service & Sales Representatives
Customer Service | Austin, TX

Apply Now

Send Jobvite

BuildASign.com is looking for an E-Customer Service & Sales Representative, specifically with at least two years of email support and sales experience with a great attitude. Our Customer Service/ Sales Team answers customer calls, emails and live chat inquiries for both pre and post-order customers. We expect each team member to be fully knowledgeable about our product suite in order to successfully cross and up-sell customers. CSRs are also expected to identify and communicate technical problems with the order process to the appropriate departments and provide feedback to the marketing department on customer requests and trends. The information our Customer Service Sales Team gleans from our customers is vital to the evolution and success of our business.

Benefits

- $14.00/hour plus bonus plan
- Medical/Dental/Life/LTD/Vision Insurance
- Paid Time Off/ Paid Holidays
- 401 (k) plan
- Frequent Company and Team Events

How much does it cost?

Let's assume you are getting paid $20 per hour (or 20 pounds/euros). You are spending 3 hours per day processing email and you want to cut it down to 1 hour per day. That means you will potentially be able to save your company $200. Assuming you spend 3 hours each day processing email. So essentially you are spending 10 hours less on email and using that same time to execute a different, higher paying task.

This will add up over the weeks and months that follow - when you change your habit. You could end up saving a lot of time and money for yourself! Remember – **Time is Money,** as they say! This is a good example!

Action Plan

1. Measure how long it takes you to process email - record 5 sessions

2. Record the average time for one week. You will use that information in another chapter

---

CHAPTER 2 – INBOX ZERO IN MINUTES

"It's your job to train those around you to be more effective and efficient" – **Timothy Ferriss**

How Many Minutes Will You Assign to Processing Email?

In the first chapter you will have worked out how much time you spend on average processing email. What was your average number? It might be 30 minutes, it might be 60 minutes. Whatever it is - ask yourself if you want to improve that use of time.

Measure Your Time

When do you typically start email? Make a written note how many emails you have unopened/unread. Make a note of what the time is and start going through your emails. Jim, how long should I spend reading an email? You should spend no more than 2 minutes per email.

Some emails will take less than 10 seconds to read as you will read and simply delete, using the *RWEF* system defined in **Chapter 13**, later on in this book. For example, if you have 60 emails and it took you 60 minutes to process the emails using the *RWEF* system you will on average be taking a minute per email. David - that makes sense right?

Can you delegate Email/tasks?

In his book The 4-Hour Workweek: Escape 9-5, Live Anywhere..," Timothy Ferriss says the last thing Entrepreneurs delegate is their email. They think, or say that email is a magic process that only they can do. Just like anything else it's a process that you learn and get better at after practice, but you can delegate email to someone else and do not have to do it yourself.

If you are an Executive, a President, or a C-suite executive the chances are you already have 2-4 people doing your email for you anyway. Learn from these people. Perhaps you could delegate your **personal email** to someone else, maybe your spouse if they like reading your email! You can even delegate to a **Virtual Assistant** (VA)!

What works in your business?

How often and how many times you read, write and respond to email will often depend on **YOU** and your customers. Test out by starting small and then increasing the delay each time you test. You could start out at 2 hours, then 4 hours, then 8 hours and so on.

Looking at this approach from another angle, if you are one of those people that responds to email as soon as it arrives in your inbox, then it will be much harder for you to change your bad habit.

Ask yourself will my boss give me a pay rise because I am the only one that answers emails in seconds. I am sure he/she would answer **NO WAY - DON'T BE ABSURD!** Also review your annual *performance objectives*. Is responding to email in there as an objective? Does it mention you must be at a certain skill level and experience in Email Management?

The chances are high that there will be no reference to it in your job description too.

For most office workers, it's expected and you don't get any extra **brownie points** for doing it! Don't spend too much time on tasks that are expected and <u>not recognized</u> as **exceptional work**.

Touch email only once

Use the touch email only once principle as much as possible. When you sit down to process your email, use the mindset to process (touch it) only once. If you leave email in your inbox you will undoubtedly open up the email again and this wastes valuable time resources you need to use elsewhere. Use my *RWEF* system.

Use either Erase, or File after you have read and written a response to the email you are processing. If you drag it to your To-Do list you will reduce your productivity in processing email.

Your To-Do List

Some email users like to drag emails they cannot respond to immediately (as they take more than a few seconds) to their task list. You may wish to do this and then delete the original email once it is in the task list of Microsoft Outlook. Just be careful though, as you may be storing your email in another place.

The more times you touch an email, the less likely you will become a productive person. Deal with it once and only once is the right way to approach your email. Google has a Task list too that you can use. You might also consider <u>Evernote</u> – many Entrepreneurs live by it on a day-to-day basis.

The Email Game

If you mainly use Gmail from Google you can also play the Email Game - go here: http://emailgame.baydin.com/learn.html You will have to give this Web App access to your Google Gmail Account though.

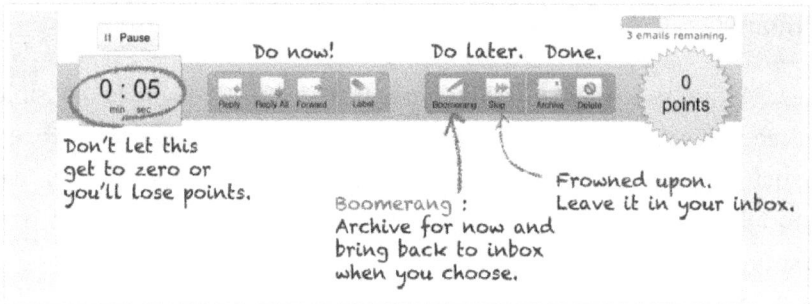

Once you have worked out how much time you spend, assign that number of minutes each day to do email. Do it once only is the GOAL!

Link to Evernote: http://evernote.com/

Action Plan

1. Delegate some email tasks to a VA, or Admin if you are a Manager/Executive.

2. Test how long it takes to do email in one sitting (batch)

3. Block out the same time on your schedule based on point 2 to process your email

---

CHAPTER 3 - WHEN IS YOUR BEST TIME TO WRITE EMAIL?

"Although your time and attention are finite, the demands on your time and attention are infinite" - **Merlin Mann**, founder of **43 folders**, discussing Inbox Zero.

The Golden Hour

These are the thoughts that first fill your mind in the morning - usually the first hour of the day, or when you wake up. In his book, **"Goals!: How to Get Everything You Want -- Faster Than You Ever Thought Possible,"** Link: http://amzn.to/Y88JCm Brian Tracy explains that this is the best time to write and review your goals.

You could use the **Golden Hour** Link: http://bit.ly/15lP57o to get your inbox. to **zero emails** when you are ready to start work. However, many experts believe you should never do email first thing in the morning. My advice to you - work on your biggest task first thing, then process your email, or if that is too hard, try spending **5-15 minutes** reviewing your action plan for the day before starting email.

Brian Tracy says, **"Every minute you spend in planning saves 10 minutes in execution; this gives you a 1,000 percent Return on Energy!"**

Your Best Time is...?

Let me start the conversation for "Best Time" to write emails by giving you an example. This is from a real conversation. The names have been changed for this book ☺.

Here is an example of a question that was asked by someone recently about processing email. It was for an office worker in a large company (100,000+ employees). Jim asked, "When is the best time to write emails?" His boss said, "Well that depends...." "Depends on what?" said Jim. The boss said, "Our Company and team members expect that you reply to email as soon as the office opens.

We are a global company and people in Asia (China, India, Malaysia etc.) are expecting a reply before they go to sleep." Jim replied, "Who did you ask in the company that told you that you must reply to emails first thing in the morning?" "Have you tested this theory?" Jim continued, "What I mean by that is, has someone actually told you that they expect an email response before they go to sleep?

I am sure if you had a reply for them to read in the next morning they would be happy with that - right?" The boss replied – "Uhh, mmm, I suppose so. I would have to try it to make sure." Jim responded by saying, "If you need help here, you can always ask a colleague what time they start doing email."

My advice when you are not sure, ask a busy person when they do email. They will be happy to help you. You might need to book time on their calendar though!

Be absolutely clear in what you ask, as you may get back an answer you were not expecting. And remember that's not someone writing email in a meeting, or spending all day with their **favorite email application open**!

Recommendation

My recommendation is for you, to write emails when you **feel** you are at your most productive level. At what time in the day do most of your tasks get completed?

This should be your **highest productive time to write email**. You can start by asking yourself one question. Mr. Man I have a question for you.. - what's that, said Mr. Man? It's simply, are you a morning person, or a night person? Then go from there.

If you like to get up early and go to bed early, my suggestion is to start first thing when you get in to the office. What I tend to do (as I am a morning person) is to write and review my action plan first then I open up email. Whether it is **Google Gmail** or **Microsoft Outlook**, I always review my action plan for the day - first thing. It takes just 15 minutes to complete.

Test to discover when you are most productive

Do this for the next 7-21 days and see how much more you get done. For example if you typically have 100 emails per morning sitting in your inbox, set a goal to get the **inbox to zero in 30-60 minutes**. Always start email when you are wide awake (drank your tea, or coffee) and are at your most productive.

Action Plan

1. Work out when is your best time to start. Write it down and start each day at this time

2. Set a time slot when you will do email. Maybe 1-3 times a day is a good start

3. Ask a busy person if they have a <u>set time</u> when they do email each day

---

CHAPTER 4 – EXPECTED RESPONSE TIME [ERT]

"Persons with comparatively moderate powers will accomplish much, if they apply themselves wholly and indefatigably to one thing at a time" – **Samuel Smiles**

ERT - pronounced ghurt, like Yoghurt!

In this exercise you will figure out how often you will process email based on responses from your customers. Ask yourself a question: When should my customers expect a response? The Answer is: Test first! Start out with the largest number of hours in between receiving the email and when you will not respond to email.

Typical Response Time

Typically this might be 24 hours. If you are managing communication with multiple countries, say China, or India and you are in the United States, 24 hours is a good start. Why read and write an email from China if they are already asleep? You also have to figure out a plan for your local office. Perhaps you might decide to process your emails in batches **between 9AM, 11AM and 3PM**.

Train your customer

Remember the quote from **Timothy Ferriss in Chapter 2**? He said it's your job to train others to be more effective and efficient! Train your correspondents, clients and colleagues to understand when they should expect email from you. Believe me, even if you radically change how you process email, they will get use to the new YOU very quickly.

How you work is largely your choice, as long as it stays within the boundaries of your company policy etc.

Remember I asked you to validate **"Who asked you to check email first thing in the morning"** in a previous chapter? Find out the answer to that by asking 5-10 people you work with. Start your new habit based on what you believe is a good <u>service level agreement</u> (SLA) Link: <u>http://bit.ly/19ypuLP</u> .

Aim HIGH and then move LOWER if necessary.

Global Clients or Colleagues

If you are based in the US office and you have colleagues, clients or customers based in China - start with the **24 hour rule**. Don't send emails from your China colleagues until the end of the day. You might want to batch them when you process them earlier along with your local region's email.

The best thing you can do is make sure they have an answer to their problem when they wake up the next day. Personal emails, you could start at 7 days, or if that is too "HIGH" you could start with 1 day.

Reply within 24 hours

There is a fine balance between replying immediately and actually responding within a day. It takes time, and it takes a whole lot of testing. Do not believe you have to reply immediately, unless the email says so in the body of the email! Once you reply immediately your customers will expect the same response time [ERT] next time. Train your customers to be more effective in what they do too.

Remember your Inbox is not an organized way of seeing other people's priorities. It's all about yours – what's important to you. Once you have figured that out you will have so much more time to work on your own priority and hence success.

Action Plan

1. Write down what you believe is an acceptable time to reply if you are the customer

2. Make a rule to process and reply to regional customers last

3. Start today with how many times per day you will sit and process your email

CHAPTER 5 - WHAT DISTRACTS YOU FROM PROCESSING EMAIL [RWEF]?

"There is more to life than just increasing its speed" **– Ghandi**

What distracts me from reading, writing, erasing and filing my email? Think about the day before you started reading this book.

Here are some of the most common distractions that people let in to their working life every day.

- Outlook New Email Popup
- Incoming Phone/Txt
- Friends/Colleagues
- Instant Message (IM)
- Casual Browsing - on the Internet (aka web surfing)
- Daydreaming
- Social Media - you are looking on your Facebook Wall, or checking your Tweets, or looking at your Google+ Friends

The most annoying distraction has got to be the **New Email Popup from Microsoft Outlook**. You could be presenting important details and your audience will even see you get new email. Turn it off! Or better still, close down your email application when presenting key information to your colleagues.

If you take the class, **Getting the Edge**, or **The Effective Edge for Professionals** (http://bit.ly/1CvYkUv) it will open your eyes to being more productive in email.

The first thing they teach you is to reduce annoying time wasting distractions. The simple stuff! Every time you get distracted you will increase your time to complete a project. In a meeting you will be less effective in engaging and adding value.

Just like a factory schedule your tasks in batches. It's more efficient if you batch the tasks into similar tasks as well.

Watching YouTube - Videos

Watching *YouTube* videos may be a distraction. This one in this book is a good distraction - though. Watch this video on **YouTube** from **Merlin Mann** of **43folders**. He gives you an example of how to process your email inbox. Click here – short link: http://bit.ly/1EgkJWa This will distract you for almost **60 minutes!**

Distractions Increase Your Time to complete a single task by up to 65%

What's your number 1 distraction from getting email done in one sitting?

Do this test today.

Write down your actions for the day. Put a "*" somewhere on the sheet, maybe next to the most important action item. Look at your watch, preferably one with a second hand, and write down next to the "*" where the second hand is, like 10 seconds. Then open up your email, look at the list of emails, as many as you can see on the screen size you are reading.

Go back to the "*" It might take you a few seconds to remind your brain where it is. Then go back to your email and try and remember which email you were focusing on. Record the seconds you just wasted doing this exercise.

Average Time spent Checking Email

The point I am making here if you are reading email on average **36 times in an hour** is how much time do you think it will take to get your email processed if you don't finish the first task you are doing, without being distracted? When you commit to writing email, you should put away all your distractions. Just keep your tools where they are needed. See [**Figure 5.1**] for example of averages.

Figure 5.1

[INFOGRAPHIC - courtesy of
http://www.atlassian.com/time-wasting-at-work-infographic]

How to Turn off Outlook Email Notifications

Watch this YouTube Video: Link: http://bit.ly/1aLp8nY or go to Microsoft's site and Turn off alerts. Link: http://bit.ly/1zY96wA

More tools, like these can be found in the Technology Tools Chapter - **Chapter 20**.

62% of respondents worldwide cited wasting time on non-essential emails as the most challenging aspect of email use. - Mimecast "The Shape of Email 2012" (2012).

Do you want to get a free ebook (may need to share your personal information to get it)?
You can get a copy of a "Guide to Avoiding 8 Time-Wasting, Deadline-Missing, Infection-Spreading Workplace Zombies" here:
http://www.workfront.com/resources/ebook/the-working-dead/

Action Plan
1. Resolve today to put away your distractions
2. Determine how many times you check Email per hour
3. Read the eBook mentioned on the previous page about workplace distractions

CHAPTER 6 - EMAIL RULES IN THE OFFICE

"We are stubborn on vision. We are flexible on details…. We don't give up on things easily." - **Jeff Bezos** "Amazon willing to be misunderstood for long periods of time" (2011).

What Email Rules do I need?

One rule that you need to stick to is - send attachments through email that are no larger than **2Mb**. Larger than that you should share on a sharing file server. See **Chapter 18** for more information on Email Etiquette.

How many folders do you need?

Less than you believe is the answer! Have you ever heard the phrase – "Less is more?" This applies to your email folders!

I have seen many email users that have elaborate lists of folders. They look pretty on the Overhead Projector (OHP), but that's as far as it goes. Less is more in my book. Getting back to the book…

Does this Clutter Make my Butt Look Fat?

Link: http://amzn.to/17QANQv if you are filing stuff in folders, you are wasting time being productive - even if it is automated. When do you have time to click that folder and review it? Just have two folders!

Same as we did back in the old days - In tray, out tray, just label them more appropriately to YOU! Maybe you could call them - "For review later," or just "Processed". Just remember - don't use too much **smart brain power** executing this!

Setup Rules to File in to Folder Categories

This is best explained by [**Figure 6.1**] on the page below. This applies to Microsoft Outlook Email, but similar rules can be set up with other applications.

Figure 6.1

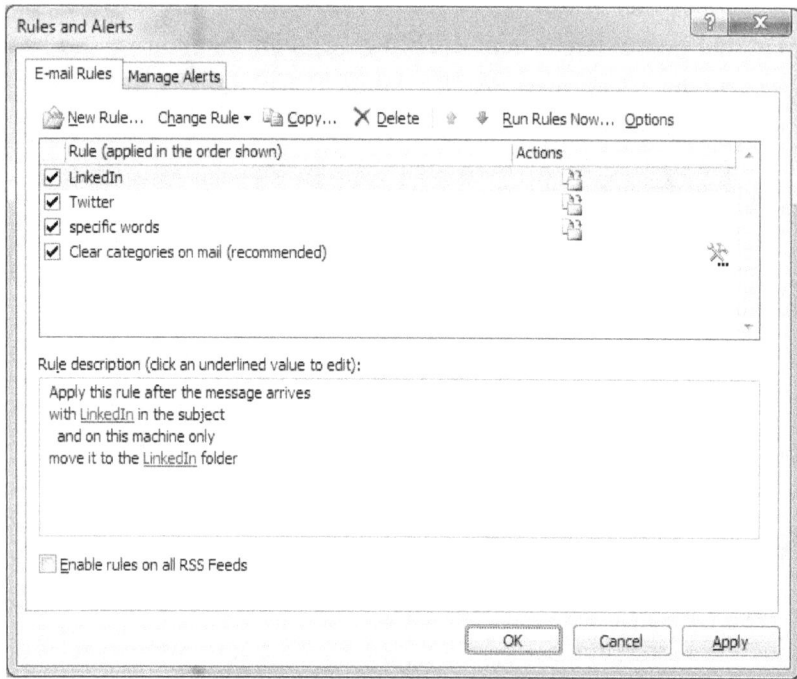

Junk & Spam Email

Setup a rule for Junk Mail. Then train your Email application. It takes time to train it to recognize what is Junk, Spam etc.

Why do we need Email Rules in the Office?

Looking at the screenshot below [**Figure 6.2**], email has become a **monster of uncontrollable work**. If you use Microsoft Outlook, your Inbox has become an organized way of presenting to you, other people's action items. The sooner you realize that, the more productive you will become.

Figure 6.2

We spend an average of **4 hours a day using email,** meaning that email impacts approximately **50%** of our working day. Adding to this, **39%** of users regularly send, receive and check emails outside working hours. - Mimecast "**The Shape of Email 2012.**"

Note: This chapter was shared on LinkedIn.com recently and got quite a few thumbs up!

Link to the LinkedIn Publisher Post: http://linkd.in/1MAruVa

Action Plan
1. Decide what rules you will put in place for your Email Application
2. How many folders do you want to create?

CHAPTER 7 - WHAT ARE YOU TRYING TO GET ACCOMPLISHED?

"An average person with average talent, ambition and education, can outstrip the most brilliant genius in our society, if that person has clear, focused goals" – **Brian Tracy**

Every time you start a new email message the content should contain actionable steps with minimum words. If you can get away with just writing the action in the Subject title then that is even better. For example you might write this.

Subject: *Lunch Today at 12PM, the usual place - Yes/No?* The subject says it all, so you really do not need to write anything in the body. You can also achieve a similar outcome using your phone too!

What's your End Goal?

Start with the end in mind. Someone once said, that if a website takes more than 8 seconds to load for a first time customer visit then they will leave and never return.

Using part of that notion you must be clear in your opening sentence what you want to communicate in the email. Follow this system when writing an email each day, especially to a new audience: S. T. A. R. T.

This means *Subject Title*, then *Action*, then *Results* and *Time* to provide the action, or results.

Recall the Who, What, How etc. from **Mr. Kipling** - if not review this YouTube Audio. Short link: http://bit.ly/18Uiqva You must point out to others, the **Who** and **What** when writing email most of the time. Obviously you can do this indirectly by learning how to make good use of To: CC: and BCC ☺.

Otherwise your potential audience might have to guess who needs to respond. This is especially important when communicating with Global teams.

Don't be shy, or you'll never get anything done quickly.

What action do you want to get from this email? Who do you want to accomplish the action? If you use the reply all, don't forget to assign someone to do something. Also common mistake is to have the person who needs to do the action on the CC: line and not To: line.

Color codes do not work well if the sender has made this error.

When do you want it by? Microsoft Outlook has great features that will pop-up a reminder if you set the Follow up, as in the screenshot [**Figure 7**]. The recipient will get a reminder if the task is past due and the email turns red!

Figure 7

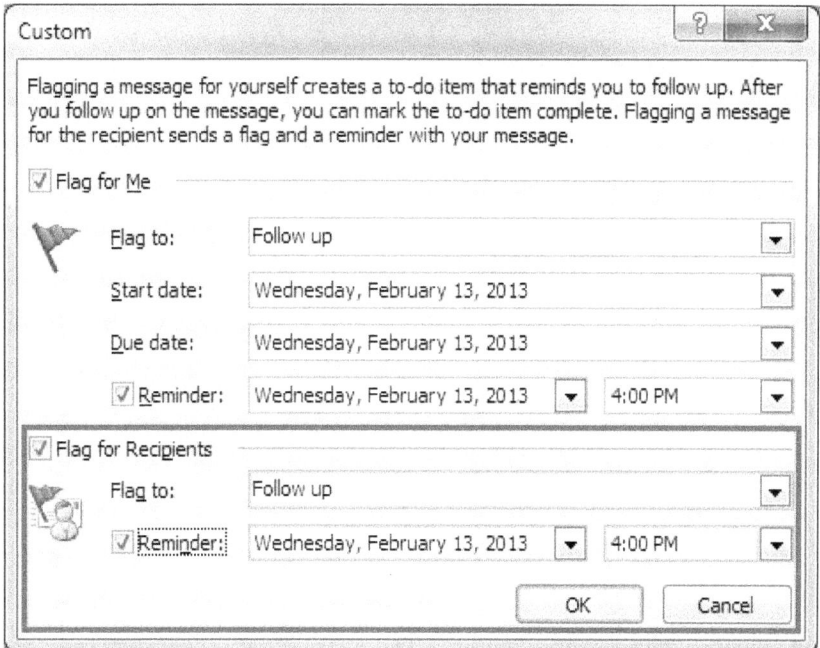

Action Plan

1. Watch the YouTube Video – type in the link on your personal computer - see the previous page
2. Find out how to use the Follow up feature for your Email application of choice

CHAPTER 8 - WHO IS YOUR AUDIENCE?

"There is one quality which one must possess to win, and that is definiteness of purpose, the knowledge of what one wants, and a burning desire to possess it" – **Napoleon Hill**

Before you write a new email, pause and think about this question. Who is going to read this email and what do I need them to know, or do? Once you have figured that out - you are ready to begin.

Try to exercise this routine by asking the question each time you read a new email.

Don't send an email, just because you can! When you are thanking someone for something they do through email…ask yourself if everyone needs to know about your compliment, or you could just send it to the person you are sending the thank you note to ☺.

Are you thinking WIIFM, or WIIFT?

Remember it's not about you, it's about them! What's In It For Them [WIIFT]! Write thinking about the customer first and how you can get inside their head with your email approach.

Who cares About You?

Only You Do! Remember that only you care about YOU when you write. When writing your email, approach your customer the same way. You care about them, because they care about themselves! Reply All - No don't do it! Stop and think first. Does everyone need to know you are Thankful?

Email Marketing

When you read the next chapter, you will get some clues on what you need to think about before writing and sending an email. When you have mastered email at your office, you will eventually have an email template for every type of audience you need to communicate with.

It can be: Execs, Peers/Team mates/Extended Team members/Girl Guides/Or any audience that you will continually communicate with on a regular basis. Just like a resume/cv each audience deserves special content! Some call these, "Email Scripts."

Action Plan

1. Create a communication plan - different categories of audience

2. Create different email templates according to the audience and communication detail. Use your communication plan

---

CHAPTER 9 - EMAIL MARKETING

"Write in a way that comes easily and naturally to you, using words and phrases that come readily to hand. But do not assume that because you have acted naturally your product is without flaw." –
E.B. White

What is Email Marketing?
Subject Title:
ACTION: What do you want the reader to do for you?
Get to the point fast!

Knowing when to deliver your message

According to the book, "How to Email Important People," the worst times you can send an email is on a **Monday or Friday**. Typically Monday is the worst time, as people usually prefer to catch up on what they missed on Friday and over the weekend. Also, when you have a Global job role, in some global regions, Monday will be your Sunday. On your Sunday you could get extra email to deal with.

Short link to the book, "How to Email Important People" – http://amzn.to/ZokJP5

Social Media Tools

These days Social Media tools can really help you understand when people read their emails, as social media accounts are a leading indicator of customer's behavior. See diagram below from The Science of Email Marketing, 2011.

Effect of Time-of-Day on Clickthrough Rate

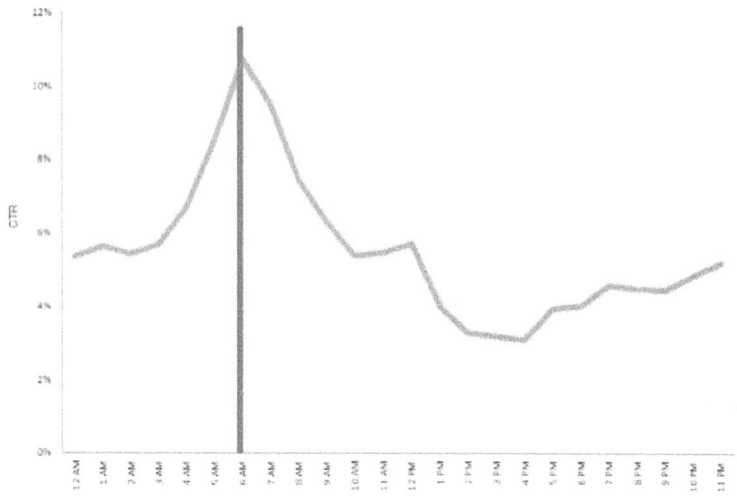

SOURCE: THE SCIENCE OF EMAIL MARKETING, 2011

From the chart above you can see that typically users are opening their email* (with links in them) around 6 AM in the morning. This is a good indicator to help you decide when you should send your most important email.

As you master email management you can schedule your email to get sent at a specified time and date. *Note chart is indicating clicks inserted through emails.

In Microsoft Outlook you can schedule the sending of email by following these steps. See next page for those instructions.

Steps to Schedule Email to be sent at a later date or time

1. Create the email, as normal
2. On the top ribbon – click the Options tab
3. On the far right click on the down arrow, **message options**
4. Click on the Do not deliver before and enter the date and time
5. See screenshot below for an example

Refer to your favorite email application to see if this feature is available to use.

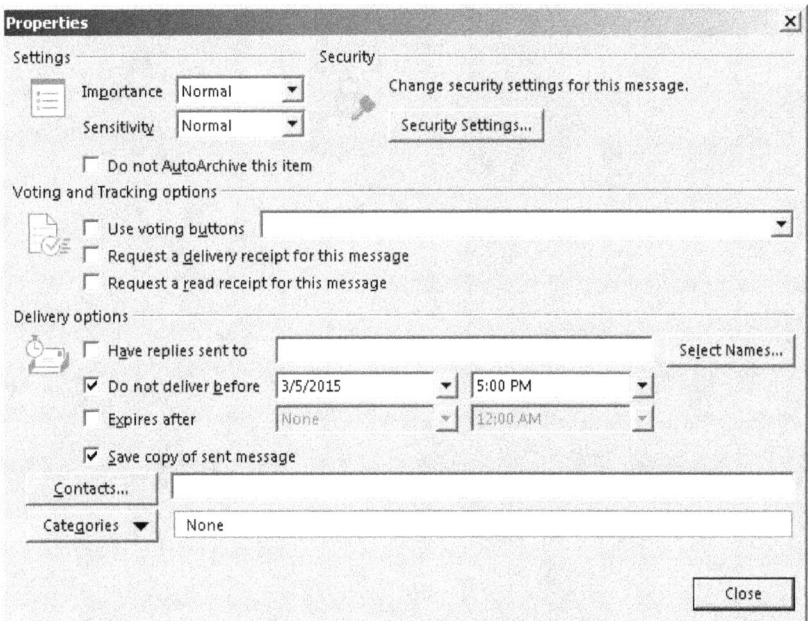

Action Plan
1. Review the section at the end of this book for more information on Email Marketing
2. Learn more about your audience. Write down the time when you are most likely get a response to your email

---

CHAPTER 10 - WHEN TO USE TO: CC: OR BCC

"All happiness depends on a leisurely breakfast" - **John Gunther**

In this chapter, I will explain an reinforce the use of these categories. Typically the BCC (Blind Carbon Copy) is hidden in some email applications. You will need to enable it to use it ☺.

Send To Fields

Explain To:
Explain CC:
Explain BCC:
Reply all - hint!

When to Use To:

This happens a lot in large companies. An email user will hit the reply all to save time typing in all the email addresses/names and then reply wanting an action from a single person. Only the person they want the action from is on the CC line. If that person, let's say Bob is not on the To: line and they have set a rule to color emails when they are on the To: Line they will not see that color coding when the email reply reaches their Inbox.

Always make sure you have the right email correspondents on either the To: Line. These are the people you want to respond to your request, or have an action to go do.

When to Use the CC: Line

When you should use the CC line - simple when you think there is someone on your team that needs a copy.

Avoid Reply to All whenever possible

Always contemplate about your audience when assessing the habit of replying to all.

There will be some people who send email to a large distribution and they will specifically tell you to reply direct and not use the reply all feature. Why do they ask you to do that?

Usually the reason they ask, is to ensure that only they get the reply and not to impact others on the distribution - **it's just that simple**.

Sending an email to everyone will just add to the problem of everyone having too much email. **9 times out of 10** they will not care about your response unless they need to do something and their name is called out on the To: line.

Stop and think before you send that email. Send emails on a need-to-know basis. If you click "Reply all" and not everyone needs to know about your message it is a **waste of resources**.

When to use BCC

You can use the BCC in at least 3 separate occasions in the office.

Short link: http://en.wikipedia.org/wiki/Blind_carbon_copy

1) When you are sending an email to a large distribution and you want to prevent your clients hitting the reply all button. You would also write some text in the email on who the email is going to in terms of world-wide regions- if applicable).

2) You wish to send a personal thank you note to a colleague's boss and you include your colleague's email address in the BCC line.

3) Protecting your customer's identity is paramount and you are sending an email to a small list of people who may not know each other. Email Marketers do this a lot.

Here is another look at Blind Carbon copy. You can research more information on the internet. For your convenience here is one link you can review below.

In Summary, think before you write, then reflect on your message before you hit the send button! This is especially important in a large company!

Refer to this link: http://huff.to/1BLD3Vs

Action Plan
1. Learn how and when to use the BCC feature by clicking on the link above
2. Copy only those that need to know, but do not need to execute an action item

CHAPTER 11 - WHAT'S YOUR OUT OF OFFICE RULE?

"And herein lies the secret of true power. Learn, by constant practice, how to husband your resources, and concentrate them, at any given moment, upon a given point" - **James Allen**

Out of Office Content

First thing first, please don't write a novel! Just get to the point very quickly. Remember *Mr. Kipling*? You just need to say **Who**, **What**, **When** etc.

Don't SPAM Me!

Ok so you are out of office, thanks for letting me know. I also appreciate it that you have notified me that you have a Backup (someone covering you) while you are out. Please don't setup a rule that sends me an email every time you are on copy, or on the To: line while you are out. I now have to manage that additional email.

Remember to think about your audience - how many people are you reaching during a typical week? Those same people will get your out-of-office email too!

So my advice to you – setup an **Out of Office** [OOO] rule, but setup another rule that keeps telling me what I already know. A top-performer will make a note you are out on their calendar, so they won't need a constant reminder!

Your Backup Is OOO Too!

This happens a lot in large companies (10,000 employees or more). You assign a Backup to cover you while you are out, but they are out as well. How helpful is that?

Thanks for the great OOO email and the lousy customer service. Make sure your backup colleague is available for the full duration of you being out!

I bet you can think of a few OOO scenarios too – right?

Action Plan

1. Turn off the rule that spam's your colleagues when you are out of the office

2. Implement a compromise – send an OOO email only once

CHAPTER 12 - COLOR-CODE YOUR EMAIL

"Colors, like features, follow the changes of the emotions" - **Pablo Picasso**

What's Your Boss Color?

Outside normal RWEF processing you also want to be able to take a few seconds glance in your Inbox and instantly know you have email from your BOSS! You can do that by selecting a color to code your emails from your BOSS! You will have to decide though from the outset if you will use this code just for your boss email to make it work.

Office Color

Here is where you can make the changes if you are using Microsoft Outlook 2010. Review this blog link - Color code your Outlook 2010 Inbox Messages. Note: The conditional formatting color I use is blue for emails that are sent directly To: Me and myself only.

Label Codes

In Google Gmail you use label codes. More can be found here - Google Help. In Thunderbird you can Google for Color code your emails and a whole list of options will come up. There are also FREE add-ons you can download and use to help you scan important emails quicker.

Typically high volume email users will implement color coding their email after they have set up rules, alerts and categories for their incoming email Inbox. I also recommend you find a friend, colleague or family member who has experience with managing multiple email accounts in the one inbox.

What's Your Favorite Color?

Is it Red, Green, Yellow, Blue or another color? Whatever it is make sure you use a color that looks good on the computer screen! Assign a color today for YOU and one for your Boss!

Action Plan

1. Click on the Color code your Outlook 2010 Inbox link and learn how to use the feature

2. Choose a color code for email that works for you and your personal/work environment

---

CHAPTER 13 - CREATE A SYSTEM [RWEF] TO PROCESS EMAIL

"Being busy does not always mean real work. The object of all work is production or accomplishment and to either of these ends there must be forethought, system, planning, intelligence, and honest purpose, as well as perspiration. Seeming to do is not doing" -
Thomas A. Edison

Read Once, Write Once, and Erase [*RWEF*]

Reduce Email Touch Points - if you do not deal with the email in the first instance you could deal with it up to 10 times before moving it out of your Inbox!

Increase your chance/speed to find email. To do that you need a system.

Create a system, like - *RWEF* [pronounced Ref!] - Read Write, Erase and File. This system is pronounced "*Ref*" because you need "someone" to remind you of the rules of the email game!

What's Your System?

This is probably the single most important part of processing email each day, week, month and year. To be successful you need a system. All successful business run on some kind of system.

You need to create a system too that you can run your business on!

I call my email system - *RWEF*. I came up with this name for several reasons:

1. I needed an acronym that I could easily remember
2. I wanted to relate to something I am passionate about - Football/Soccer. The RWEF, is pronounced "Ref" and in Soccer we tend to make the Ref the extra (Wo)man on the pitch! *RWEF* can be your extra IT person helping you process your email - FASTER!

3. The acronym should dictate the order that you process email

Read, then **Write**, then **Erase** and then finally **File** what you are working on. If you are not going to respond, then skip the Write part of the process and simply erase!

Action Plan
1. Read once, write once and then erase
2. Develop an email management system that you can implement in your work environment

---

CHAPTER 14 - TOO MANY FOLDERS!

"Don't limit yourself. Many people limit themselves to what they think they can do. You can go as far as your mind lets you. What you believe, remember, you can achieve" - **Mary Kay Ash**

What's a good number of folders to have to file Email?

Experiment with a paper filing system - layout 10 folders - then 5, then 2 etc.

Test your folder system. Will it work with...

SEO/Search – can your reduce search time?

Minimize extra work by using folder categories that make sense.

Remember the more folders and the Hierarchy+35% rule.

One or Two Folders

How many folders do you really need in Outlook or Gmail? The answer is really one! Two folders if you must - one called Processed and another Unprocessed. I will explain more in detail shortly. I use to have many folders - like 40+ but since Microsoft bought the fastest search engine on the planet for finding email (Lookout) I shifted gears.

Now Windows 7 and Outlook 2010 find documents and emails lightning fast. Read more about Lookout here - Lookout!
Short Link: http://bit.ly/ZokSC1

Wasting Time

Too much time is spent looking for stuff in life. Email can be included too. You spend more time looking for stuff if you have more folders. Prevent this bad habit by not hoarding, or creating too many folders.

The next chapter will help you decide what to file. Since you only have 1 or 2 folders this should not be a problem now!

Test a Paper Filing System

Before you get started with an electronic filing system...
Get 10 Manila folders and lay them out on your desk or the floor. Get 10 sheets of paper and label them 1 through 10. Then put 1 sheet of paper in each folder. Label each Manila folder with the number corresponding to the sheet enclosed. Now shuffle the folders so they are not in number sequence.

Take out all the sheets and then put them back in different folders. Find number 5. Time how long it takes you to find the number 5 piece of paper. You get the point - right? Reduce to 2 folders and have the same number of sheets - you will find the number 5 much faster. Remember people spend 35% of their time looking for stuff - which is a big waste of time. Do what you can to reduce this bad time wasting habit!

Discipline is Key

Limit what you search for and how you spend your time. Need a plan? The Zenhabits offline website will help you there. Link can be found here: http://zenhabits.net/offline/
Review the Question - Am I wasting my time organizing email? A study of email refinding.
Short Link can be found here: http://bit.ly/1FASCOU

Action Plan
1. Merge all your folders into one, or two folders
2. Record how much time you spend looking for emails with your current folder setup

---

CHAPTER 15 - TO FILE OR NOT TO FILE?

"If you ask me to play myself, I will not know what to do. I do not know who or what I am." - **Peter Sellers**

Interesting facts about filing

- 35% of time is wasted looking for stuff
- 60% of stuff filed is never reviewed ever again
- 90% of Employees save more documents than they actually need to

When to file email over hitting delete?

If you want to file something you also need a strategy whether you want to store any attachments in your email, or strip attachment, file it in your data filing system, then delete the email that had the attachment.

According to **Contural**, "Over 90 percent of employees save more documents than they actually need to, which results in enormous storage and retrieval problems. Solving this kind of hoarding requires a sound information governance strategy that accommodates for employees' work habits."

If you are a hoarder at home, then chances are you will exhibit the same behavior in your Inbox. Don't do it. Learn to just carry what you are wearing on your back! Travel light you will feel much better – believe me. I suggest you read Peter Walsh's book "Does this Clutter Make my Butt Look Fat?" Short Link: http://bitly.com/12LKsBu

If your home is cluttered, or you are a collector of things, or a hoarder – go check out Peter Walsh on Amazon.com for more of his books on his comment on diets and wanting a life you deserve. The same goes for your Inbox! You don't want a FAT Inbox. As **Peter Walsh** says, "The easiest thing to be in America is fat."

Email Application Features that can reduce your habit of filing

Hit the **delete button** - that's an easy one. You can cut out the steps below if you decide to use the delete button!

Steps Removed

1) Reading;
2) Writing and
3) Filing.

Microsoft Outlook has a feature called Mailbox Cleanup. In the application - Microsoft Outlook 2010 (works the same way in Outlook 2013) you can access it by:

1) Clicking File,
2) Then clicking Info,
3) Clicking Cleanup tools,
4) Click Clean up tools – Mailbox cleanup

In Outlook 2013 you access it from the Home Tab and it is in the delete section.

You can also use Microsoft Conversation Clean up to eliminate redundant messages too. Here is the link: Conversation Clean up.
Short Link: http://bit.ly/1wUizcE

Thanks to my good friend, former Premier Over 30 Soccer/Football team goalie: Brian Osborne for the tip! His LinkedIn Profile Link: http://lnkd.in/zkpTrk

Action Plan

1. If you use Microsoft Outlook go and find out how to use it. Click on the link above

2. Develop a new habit – stop storing data that you will never read – delete it now!

CHAPTER 16 - WHEN NOT TO WRITE EMAIL

"We often discover what will do by finding out what will not do; and probably he who never made a mistake never made a discovery" - **Samuel Smiles**

Here are Times you should not write an email

On my whiteboard in my office I have 3 common methods of communicating information, or getting information from others.

1) Email
2) Phone
3) Meeting

I base that priority on cost, distance, speed and impact. You should do the same. Sometimes it is better to write an email, but as you know it is faster to talk than write email. So sometimes the old fashion way of communicating (not texting, or emailing) - you should revert to picking up the phone.

7 Reasons to avoid Writing Emails

1) When speed is important and a phone call will work
2) When it's possible that the recipient will not read the email (late Friday/over the weekend)
3) When you need to communicate an important message that requires body language and tone
4) When the person is sitting behind you!
5) When you haven't reviewed your action items first thing in the morning
6) When you are able to Delegate the task. Even if you don't have a VA/Admin/Secretary there are still times where you can practice this management skill
7) When you need to have a conversation

There is another point I should make that requires your attention. **You absolutely do not need to respond to every email you receive**. Learn the <u>80/20 Principle</u> and apply it in all areas of your life. Short Link to 80/20 principle - http://bit.ly/1AblMAy

If you are responding to every email today, you should attempt to change that habit. Since this is a personal choice for everyone you should have the common sense to know when not to respond, or process an email.

You should also avoid writing an email when you have a "sense" that there will be a lot of back and forth in resolving an issue that could be easily resolved with one phone call, or meeting.

Very Important

Referring back to **7 Reasons to avoid Writing Emails**, Emails are documents and not conversations. **See point 7** on **page 63**.

We have gotten so good at writing a quick email, rather than pick-up the telephone, or walking down to the person's office that we might believe an email is a conversation.

These days, emails can last forever and can be easily forwarded, copied, printed, faxed etc. To avoid this situation, ask yourself – Do I mind if this email was printed in a national, or local newspaper?

Would you want everyone to read it? Stop and ask yourself this question. Make it your new habit before writing and hitting the send button.

Reality Check

The convenience of email can lead to its overuse. Emails are best for communicating simple, straightforward factual information. It can be more efficient and effective to discuss complex or sensitive issues by phone or in person.

Action Plan

1. Write down your communication plan – put it on your whiteboard in your cube

2. Decide today which emails you will no longer respond to

3. Print out a list of reasons when you should avoid sending an email

CHAPTER 17 - WHEN TO WRITE PERSONAL EMAILS?

"The odd thing about this form of communication is that you're more likely to talk about nothing than something. But I just want to say that all this nothing has meant more to me than so many somethings" You've Got Mail - 1998 [Movie].

Writing Personal Emails at Work

At a recent conference (DellWorld) Bill Clinton mentioned how many emails he sent when he was President. Can you guess it was only two! One to the troops serving in the Balkans/Bosnia and 1 to John Glen when he was up in Space at the age of 77. Most of the email was interoffice traffic. People would type before they thought.

See minute 43 in the YouTube video link:

http://www.youtube.com/watch?v=DzXrKtQghUY

What's Your Company Email/Communication Policy?

If you work for a large company (10,000+ people) there will undoubtedly be a note advising you of the company's Information Technology (IT) policy.

Also many companies ensure you see their **Email/Communication policy** (the main points) every time you logon to your company network. Did you look at it recently? Go check it out today!

Read your client's/company policy about email. You will be surprised by how many tips you will get in there on how to act and present yourself when writing email. Read and act as if you were paying the bills and you'll definitely act differently!

Time Away from Work - not doing what you are paid for. When you are on holiday/vacation – do you check your office email?

Always ask yourself this question – If I was the CEO and I was paying the bills would I be impressed with my staff spending time doing stuff they are not getting paid to do? Think like a Top-Performer! Work all the time you work. When it's time to leave the office, leave and have fun! If you need someone to coach and guide you find a mentor . You will find many on LinkedIn! Tap in to your company network.

Note: Dellworld can be found here: http://www.dellworld.com

Action Plan
1. Go find out what your company Email Management Policy is
2. Review the YouTube Video presentation from President Bill Clinton

---

CHAPTER 18 - EMAIL ETIQUETTE

"Leadership is the ability to get extraordinary achievement from ordinary people" **– Brian Tracy**

Quick Fire - Email Etiquette

Here is a quick fire list of all the things you need to consider when writing emails to your customers.

What is civility? – it could be the respect of other people's time. Time Wasters! Who are they?

Subject Title! What has this got to do with what you are currently discussing?

Someone who spams you with their OOO Rule…

Email Users who make you read the whole email instead of copying the latest content to the top of the email

Reply All - When someone makes a mistake by sending an email to a Global Email Group (in Outlook) it's called: Don't compound that mistake by asking to be taken off the list! You are just adding to the extra emails

Respect the Meeting Organizer

I regularly attend meetings with team members at my client's campus and you will not believe how many people are dis-engaged in the meeting. They are either writing email, or checking their smart phone, or even worse browsing the internet and reading the news.

THIS HAS TO STOP NOW! This is SO RUDE! Be Nice to your fellow colleague.

Engage today and tomorrow – in everything you do! You will be glad and happy that you did!

I find that through experience, the only person who is engaged tends to be the one that organized the meeting. Leave your phone in your car, or locked in your office drawer. If you calculate the hourly rate of everyone in the room and then get billed for wasting all these team members time, you would soon stop this behavior!!! IBM use to do this – apparently.

Remove me from the Global Mail List

This happens a lot in large companies, such as Microsoft, Google, Dell, Hewlett Packard and many more etc. An email user will request to be removed from the email list. For example they may send an email to the Group list with a Subject of: Can you remove me from the mailing list of "Global Group Name Mailing List."

So depending on how large the Global list is, every member of that group will get the same email that got sent out.

If there are members in the list from China, Ireland, Poland and other countries, everyone will get that same email! The correct procedure to follow is…

1) Use the Mail Properties (usually called Outlook Properties) and the Group will have an owner.
2) Send a direct message to that Group Admin and not the whole list.
3) Then ask them to remove you from the list

Email Attachments

First of all, attach the attachment if you mention it. Sometimes we forget to attach the file we mention in the body of the email. I know I have! Some email applications will catch this.

Size is also an issue when sending large files. This is kind of an issue for some, since large companies tend to limit the size of email boxes (PST) on Exchange Servers.

This is assuming you are a Microsoft Office Company. Your company mainly installs and creates documents in Microsoft Office Product applications.

My general rule on this is, do not send your colleagues file sizes larger than 2Mb. When you are working in a global company the more people that do not adhere to this rule, the more chance you will not be able to send email because you received a large file attachment that puts your inbox size over that IT setting.

Now - do you really want your Inbox is full of large file attachments?

Calendar Attachments

Similar to Email attachments, when your calendar invite has an attachment to it that is 1MB or more you should send an invite after the meeting to remove the attachment. By doing this you can help your customers as well as your Corporate IT team to reduce calendar sizes. Sometimes Outlook Calendar will hang due to the large file size of your Calendar file.

File Share or Microsoft SharePoint

Instead of embedding the attachment, what you should do is send a link to the attachment. Again if you are a Microsoft Office User you can upload the attachment to a Microsoft SharePoint Server. Outside of Microsoft there are plenty of options available to you for sharing large files – like box.net and Google docs etc. Please don't send large file attachments in email!

IT Issues

If you are someone who is fortunate enough to manage IT issues and you have a Global centralized database for tracking issues...please make sure you use that Issue Tracker database and not email! I find that many people end up discussing issues in email, sending very important data through email, but they forget to upload those log files to the Issue Tracker.

Again please think outside of your Inbox – we need access to the log files 24/7 for anyone that has that access. What good is the tool if we are not using it for its intended purpose!

Color

Make your emails pleasing to your audience. Use color wisely. Many companies use Red when there is an issue and there is no solution to implement, or is not known at the time of reporting the issue in email. So be aware of what you are reporting.

The default color for Emails that are due is Red (the **Follow Up** Feature) for Microsoft Outlook makes that happen.

Thank You!

It's important to thank the person who has completed a task for you. However, please make sure you send the thank you note to the person you are thanking and not the whole list. If not, you just created extra work for all those people included on the email list.

Action Plan

1. Choose 3 of these Email Etiquettes and decide today which ones you will implement
2. Most importantly – say thank you whenever possible to your customers

CHAPTER 19 - GET AN EMAIL MENTOR

"Effective executives, in my observation, do not start with their tasks. They start with their time. And they do not start out with planning. They start by finding out where their time actually goes. Then they attempt to manage their time and to cut back unproductive demands on their time. Finally they consolidate their "discretionary" time into the largest possible continuing units..." **– Peter Drucker**

Find an Email Mentor

Find a busy person - remember the rule!

Rule: Work will always get done fast by a busy person!

Test, Test and Test!

What do these busy people do with their email? How do they process email? Set up a 1on1 meeting with them and ask them the questions.

Send them this survey and see what their response is.

Link to survey: http://www.surveymonkey.com/s/S3XZ3BB

Interview them. Listen to what they say! Act on their advice if you believe in it.

Further Reading

You can learn a lot from reading books - in fact by reading self-development books you will undoubtedly be in the top 3% of Advanced Learners. You can start by reading other Email books on Email Management. I recommend you read the Email Marketing books first.

Why?

Well you will see how Marketers entice you to read their emails and get you to take action - aka buy their products! Here is an example below.

Subject Title: Gold in You Inbox

What do you think the open rate was for that email subject title? Quick answer – a lot!

Use the same approach in your professional and business life. See Further Reading section for potential books to add to your **Amazon Wish List**, or **Amazon Lending Library**. If you are an Amazon Prime member you can borrow and read books for FREE*, just like a traditional library.

Here is my interview review list to find someone who can help you process your email better.

1) How many times a day do you process email?
2) Do you ever leave the office some days believing you have gotten nothing done?
3) What system do you use to process email?

For more information and tips on finding someone suitable to help you improve processing email, review this surveymonkey list I created.

Link to survey: http://www.surveymonkey.com/s/S3XZ3BB

Action Plan
1. Schedule time on your Email calendar to interview someone to be your Email Mentor
2. Take and Review the Email Management survey

*No additional charge - after you have paid the Annual Prime Membership fee. Keep in mind too, that Amazon.com occasionally provides a 30 day trial membership for free.

CHAPTER 20 - TECHNOLOGY TOOLS

"Nothing can add more power to your life than concentrating all of your energies on a limited set of targets" - **Nido Qubein**

General List of Tools

The Cost of Doing Nothing Calculator - What's the cost of Doing Nothing in your business? Short link: http://bit.ly/1b4FPuE

http://goodtodo.com - this is an online To-do list that helps you get your inbox to zero quicker. Essentially it improves your productivity. You can sign up for Free.

http://evernote.com- Timothy Ferriss, the Author of "The 4-Hour Workweek" uses this tool as do many other Entrepreneurs who need to be highly productive!

http://taskrabbit.com - From To-Do, to Done!

https://www.rescuetime.com/ - Timothy Ferriss uses this to block off all Social Media sites

Centralize Mail from Different Accounts

Google Mail Fetcher - You can download mail from up to 5 different email accounts.

Google Labs - add extra features to your Google Gmail. See below screenshot [**Figure 20**]. See page 82

DropBox - You get 2GB to store your stuff: docs; photos etc.

Figure 20.

General   Labels   Inbox   Accounts and Import   Filters   Forwarding and POP/IMAP   Chat   Web Clips   Labs
Gmail Labs is a testing ground for experimental features that aren't quite ready for primetime. They may **change**, **break** or **disappear** at any time.

If (when) a Labs feature breaks, and you're having trouble loading your inbox, there's an escape hatch. Use https://mail.google.com/mail/?labs=0.

Search for a lab: gadget   e.g. search, gadget, preview

Save Changes   Cancel

Available Labs

Add a gadget by its URL: [ ] Add	**Add any gadget by URL** by Dan P and Dong C	○ Enable ◉ Disable
	Adds a "Gadgets" tab to Settings, where you'll be able to specify the URL of any gadget. This gadget will show in a box in the left column.	Send feedback
Today (Tue, Jul 29) 9a Dr. Appointment	**Google Calendar gadget** by Ben K and Garry B	○ Enable ◉ Disable

The complete list of short links to these tools are below.

- The Cost of Doing Nothing - http://bit.ly/1E1C8Nm
- A Free todo list - http://goodtodo.com
- Evernote - http://evernote.com
- What do you need help with? - http://taskrabbit.com
- Find your ideal work-life balance - https://www.rescuetime.com/
- Check email from other accounts using Gmail - http://bit.ly/1GyV1NC
- Tips and tricks from Google's Gmail team and friends - http://bit.ly/1Hp4iW7
- Your stuff, anywhere - https://www.dropbox.com/

Action Plan

1. Go check out http://evernote.com

2. Go check out Google Labs and see if there is an app that can improve your Email Management!

CHAPTER 21 – EMAIL GOALS

"Goals should be written in the following format. They should use the 3 P's. This means they should be a) Positive, b) Written in the Present tense and c) Personal" **– Patrick Gallagher**

3 Goals To Get You Started in your new and advanced email habit!

Take time off

Once a week decide to do less email. Maybe Friday don't write any emails at all. Instead use the phone, or walk down to someone you need information from instead of sending email. It's amazing the impact when one region in a Global company is on holiday.

For example when the US has Spring Break, or the Chinese celebrate Chinese New Year! The email can be reduced as much as 50% or greater!

Imagine if people did less email - it would be the same as a sales/company region taking a vacation! It only takes a few people to Lead and others will follow! Make a pledge to get started today. You could take the lead and decide today to do less email.

Simple - do less email

Email once a day, or once a week. That is the ultimate goal. Personal emails you can certainly filter down to once a week. If you can't make the change immediate you can certainly take baby steps at first.

How do you eat an elephant? The answer is...one bite at a time. You can apply the same principle in making changes to your daily/weekly email habits. Do it now and get started today.

Time to Do Email

Set a time to do email each day, each week and each month. My recommendation is to run your RWEF system at 9AM, 11AM and 3PM.

You might want to process your email when you are at your best. Some people hit the ground running in the morning and some later on in the afternoon. Whatever works for you and your business will be the way to go.

Action Plan

1. Plan 1 day a week where you will use the phone instead of writing an email

2. Decide which times are best for you to start and process email

---

SOURCES - FURTHER READING AND REFERENCE BOOKS

Some of these sources are books that I have read and some are websites that I recommend reviewing for further information. I have included links to my online Amazon Book Library

"The 4-Hour Workweek: Escape 9-5, Live Anywhere..," by **Timothy Ferriss.**
Link: http://bitly.com/180slKA

"The Effective Executive: The Definitive Guide to Getting the Right Things Done," by **Peter Drucker**.
Link: http://amzn.to/15TDXzm

"Email Marketing: An Hour a Day," by **Jeanniey Mullen**.
Link: http://amzn.to/14gzoPQ

"Bit Literacy: Productivity in the Age of...," by **Mark Hurst**.
Link: http://amzn.to/11oFd8b

"Never Check E-Mail in the Morning..," by **Julie Morgenstern**.
Link: http://amzn.to/11IvH06

"Guide to Not Checking Email," by **Jared Goralnick**.
Link: http://awayfind.com/

"Email Marketing That Sells...," by **Robert Coorey**.
Link: http://amzn.to/14WhUcc

"How to Email Important People," by **Krissy Brady**.
Link: http://amzn.to/ZAgYHe

"E-Mail: A Write It Well Guide," by **Janis Fisher Chan**.
Link: http://amzn.to/12NqshV

"Daily Inbox Zero: 9 Proven Steps to Eliminate Email Overload," by **S.J. Scott**.
Link: http://amzn.to/18bxCDf

Note: My Amazon Book Library short link is shared with you below.
Link: http://bit.ly/V63kWP

RECOMMENDED WEBSITES FOR FURTHER REVIEW

Web: The History of Email – http://en.wikipedia.org/wiki/Email

Web: Email Topics from 43 Folders – http://www.43folders.com/topics/email

Web: 120 Awesome Marketing Stats, Charts & Graphs, downloadable from hubspot.com
Link: http://bit.ly/1BsVHRt

Web: Get Away from Your Inbox
Link: http://awayfind.com/

Web: 43 Folders - Finding the best time and attention to do your best creative work
Link: http://www.43folders.com/

Web: You are not your Inbox
Link: http://bit.ly/1D7WR76

Web: http://www.amazon.com/dp/0142000280/ - Getting Things done, a book on Amazon

Web: Lost in Email...
Link: http://nyti.ms/1HGaXva

Web: 43 Folders Series: Inbox Zero - Inbox Zero - Action-based Email
Link: http://www.43folders.com/izero

Web: Effective Edge - http://effectiveedge.com/

OTHER BOOKS BY THE AUTHOR

LinkedIn Secrets Revealed: 10 Secrets To Unlocking Your Complete Profile on LinkedIn.com - http://amzn.to/12pyCNu

Publishing a Book on Amazon: 7 Steps to Publishing your #1 Book on Amazon Kindle in Minutes!
http://amzn.to/18i9JI3

Build Your Own Living Revocable Trust: A Pocket Guide to Creating a Living Revocable Trust
http://amzn.to/1CoNUmn

Spirituality in the Workplace: A Study Guide for Business Leaders
http://amzn.to/1CoNUmn

Trapped in a Meritocracy: Cracking the Meritocracy Code: Get Paid More for Valued Performance
http://amzn.to/1zbufrW

Amazon Secrets Revealed: How To Sell More Books on Amazon.com
http://amzn.to/1EBhY1O

Note: All these links are to Amazon.com eBooks. You can change the sales region, by changing .com to .co.uk etc.

QUESTIONS OR COMMENTS?

Do you Need to ask me a question and get an instant response? Email me @ LinkedInSecretsRevealed@gmail.com

I read and answer all emails sent to me, myself! I do not outsource, or crowd source this task!

EASTER EGG FUN

Let's pretend it's Easter for a moment!

If you bought this book at a **Half Price Books Store** in Austin, Cedar Park, or Round Rock, Texas I will personally send you a kindle copy of two other titles I have published.

Just email me a copy of your receipt with **Subject: Easter Egg & EMAIL INBOX MANAGEMENT BOOK PURCHASE**.

That's all I need.

Check-out Half Price Books Stores here: http://www.hpb.com/

Email me your receipt @ LinkedInSecretsRevealed@gmail.com

ABOUT THE AUTHOR

Patrick Gallagher provides his talent & services to a major Fortune 50 company and has spent hours and hours reading, training, learning from others about Email Management. Patrick has studied countless books, tested the effect of processing email in batches using Microsoft Outlook Email as well as Google Email [Gmail]. The most recent course he has studied was, "**Getting The Edge**."

Everything that is shared with you in this book is shared to help you spend more quality time with your friends and family. When Patrick is not at work he enjoys spending time in his garden and playing tennis with his eldest daughter.

Patrick is active in community affairs and regularly volunteers for local charities in the USA. He is originally from the United Kingdom and is married to his beautiful wife. They have three young children. He currently lives and works in Sunny, Texas. Where there are only two seasons: **Warm season** and **hot season**!

You can also connect with Patrick on his Twitter page, short link: http://bit.ly/Odcjqa